Date: 7/2/21

J BIO RAPINOE
Scarbrough, Mary Hertz,
Megan Rapinoe /

MEGAN RAPINOE

Women in Sports

MARY HERTZ SCARBROUGH

Rourke
Educational Media

A Division of
Carson
Dellosa
Education

Before Reading: *Building Background Knowledge and Vocabulary*

Building background knowledge can help children process new information and build upon what they already know. Before reading a book, it is important to tap into what children already know about the topic. This will help them develop their vocabulary and increase their reading comprehension.

Questions and Activities to Build Background Knowledge:

1. Look at the front cover of the book and read the title. What do you think this book will be about?
2. What do you already know about this topic?
3. Take a book walk and skim the pages. Look at the table of contents, photographs, captions, and bold words. Did these text features give you any information or predictions about what you will read in this book?

Vocabulary: *Vocabulary Is Key to Reading Comprehension*

Use the following directions to prompt a conversation about each word.

- Read the vocabulary words.
- What comes to mind when you see each word?
- What do you think each word means?

> **Vocabulary Words:**
> - activist
> - artificial turf
> - forward
> - hat trick
> - overtime
> - penalty shoot-out

During Reading: *Reading for Meaning and Understanding*

To achieve deep comprehension of a book, children are encouraged to use close reading strategies. During reading, it is important to have children stop and make connections. These connections result in deeper analysis and understanding of a book.

Close Reading a Text

During reading, have children stop and talk about the following:

- Any confusing parts
- Any unknown words
- Text to text, text to self, text to world connections
- The main idea in each chapter or heading

Encourage children to use context clues to determine the meaning of any unknown words. These strategies will help children learn to analyze the text more thoroughly as they read.

When you are finished reading this book, turn to the next-to-last page for **After Reading Questions** and an **Activity**.

TABLE OF CONTENTS

ALWAYS PLAYING

Three-year-old Megan Rapinoe thought her big brother was the coolest. She would race along the sidelines at his soccer games with her twin sister, Rachael. Their mom was the coach.

The three siblings played soccer for hours on the field near their home in Redding, California. When they were five, the sisters joined a soccer club.

REDDING, CALIFORNIA

As she got older, Megan's love of sports got stronger, but also more complicated. By sixth grade, her friends had all moved on to other interests.

"I was just lost," she said. "Sports were my whole identity."

"I wouldn't have survived without [Rachael]."

Megan kept her passion for sports and participated in soccer, basketball, and track.

Family Matters

Megan and Rachael are the youngest of six kids. Even when her talent became obvious, Megan's parents never pressured her to play sports. They only wanted her to have fun.

Left to right: Rachael, Megan, and their mom

BECOMING THE WORLD'S BEST

Not only was Megan a superb soccer player, she was also an excellent student. She won a full scholarship at the University of Portland in the state of Oregon.

Megan's college career was outstanding—when she was healthy. A knee injury kept her from playing for almost an entire season. Knee injuries would continue to be a problem in Megan's career, but that wouldn't stop her!

Megan started her professional soccer career as a **forward** right after college. She didn't limit herself to teams in the United States. She has also played for teams in Australia and France. In 2013, she joined the Tacoma, Washington, soccer team, Reign FC.

forward (FOR-wurd): a player in basketball, soccer, and hockey who plays in an attacking position and tries to score goals

Megan also plays for the U.S. Women's National Team (USWNT). Players from all over the country are on this team. They represent the U.S. in international women's soccer, including at the Women's World Cup. Megan is one of the team's captains.

Megan and Alex Morgan co-captained the USWNT in 2019.

Every four years, the Women's World Cup determines the best women's soccer team in the world. Megan played in the 2011, 2015, and 2019 World Cups. In 2011, she helped take the U.S. to the finals, where they placed second against Japan after a last-minute **penalty shoot-out**.

penalty shoot-out (PEN-uhl-tee SHOOT-out): a way of deciding a winner in the case of a tie; each team takes turns taking a certain number of kicks

Japan blocks the U.S. shot during the penalty shoot-out at the FIFA Women's World Cup final in 2011.

Not Afraid of the Spotlight

Megan is known for her energetic and enthusiastic personality. After making a goal at the 2011 World Cup, she grabbed a microphone and started to sing. Another attention grabber? Her hair. She has dyed it pink and purple.

Megan and her USWNT teammates played Japan again in the finals of the 2012 Olympics. Just like they did in the 2011 World Cup, the teams battled fiercely. This time, the U.S. won in **overtime**. Megan scored three goals for the U.S. in the Olympics that year.

overtime (OH-vur-time): extra time added to a game or competition because the score was tied at the end of normal play

Megan and her teammates won gold in the 2012 Olympics in London, England.

Score! Carli Lloyd celebrates a goal against Japan in the opening minutes of this 2015 World Cup game.

At the 2015 World Cup, the USWNT beat Japan to win the championship. Megan assisted her teammate, Carli Lloyd, in a goal during the first three minutes, making it the fastest **hat trick** in Women's World Cup history.

hat trick (hat trik): scoring three goals in one game by a single player

Megan had knee surgery in late 2015. Her spot on the 2016 Olympic team was in doubt. Megan kept her spot on the USWNT, though she was not at full strength.

For the first time in Olympic history, the USWNT failed to make it to the semifinals of a major tournament.

Losing with Grace

Megan commented after losing: "We're gracious, and…humble, and we play the game a certain way whether we win or lose. Let's do something good… Let's inspire…Let's be fierce."

The USWNT won the championship again at the 2019 World Cup. Megan received the Golden Ball Award, which is given to the best player in the tournament. Her energy on the field contributed to more people watching the Women's World Cup on television and online than ever before. More than one billion people tuned in!

More Fame

Megan received the Golden Boot award for scoring the most goals (six) during the tournament. Her biggest honor in 2019 was winning the Ballon d'Or. This is awarded to the best female soccer player in the world. She is only the second-ever recipient.

Megan celebrates in the final game of the 2019 World Cup in France.

PAYING IT FORWARD

Megan believes she has a duty to put her fame to good use. She wants to leave the game *"in a better place, and hopefully the world in a better place."*

These aren't empty words to Megan. She's an **activist** both on and off the field.

activist (ak-TIV-ist): a person who uses actions to support one side of a controversial issue

Megan and her teammates were honored in New York City following their 2019 World Cup victory.

Megan is a leader in a lawsuit seeking equal pay for women. Female soccer players earn less per game than male players. Twenty-eight women players, including Megan, are taking this to court.

They're also arguing against working conditions such as **artificial turf**, which can cause injuries. Megan has spoken out about discrimination in many areas, such as medical treatment, coaching, travel, and training.

artificial turf (ahr-tuh-FISH-uhl turf): synthetic fibers that are made to look like natural grass, usually used on playing fields

Megan is gay. Her family and community were accepting when she told them. However, knowing that many LGBTQ people experience abuse, Megan is an outspoken advocate for equal rights. She feels a responsibility to make a positive impact with the fame that has come from her soccer success.

THANKS, MOM!

At an award ceremony in 2019, Megan thanked her mother. She said her mother had instilled in her and her siblings the absolute importance of kindness and caring.

Memory Game

Look at the pictures. What do you remember reading on the pages where each image appeared?

Index

After Reading Questions

1. Did your understanding of what it takes to be one of the greatest athletes in the world change after reading this book? Explain.

2. Did you learn anything about Megan that surprised you?

3. What makes Megan successful and inspiring?

4. What are two issues that Megan has spoken out about off the field?

5. Outside of being the best soccer player she can be, what does Megan see as her duty in this world?

Activity

Megan is a very decorated soccer player. She has won tons of awards! Research some awards soccer players can receive. Which one would you like to get if you played professional soccer?

About the Author

Mary Hertz Scarbrough loved learning about Megan Rapinoe for this book. She admires Megan's excellence as an athlete and her strong commitment to issues she's passionate about. Mary writes from her home in South Dakota, where she lives with her husband and two rescue dogs. She tries to make the world a better place through volunteer work, advocacy on issues she believes in, and voting in every election.

www.rourkeeducationalmedia.com

Quote sources: Das, Andrew. "Megan Rapinoe Digs In After Trump Criticism: 'I Stand by the Remarks.'" The New York Times. The New York Times, June 27, 2019: https://www.nytimes.com/2019/06/27/sports/soccer/megan-rapinoe-trump-white-house.html. ; ESPN. "Megan Rapinoe Critical of Hope Solo Calling Sweden 'Cowards'." ABC News, August 25, 2016: https://abcnews.go.com/Sports/megan-rapinoe-critical-hope-solo-calling-sweden-cowards/story?id=41650228. ; Rapino, Megan, Rachael Rapino, Carmelina Moscato, and Lori Lindsey. "Here's to the Tomboys: By Megan Rapinoe." The Players' Tribune. The Players' Tribune, April 7, 2016: https://www.theplayerstribune.com/en-us/articles/megan-rapinoe-uswnt-soccer-tomboys

PHOTO CREDITS: page 4-5: ©serg3d, ©Olga Turkas; page 6-7: ©2018 FSTOP123, ©FayesVision/WENN.com; page 9: ©Icon Sports Media Inc. (Icon SMI) All Rights Reserved; page 10-11: ©Alan Schwartz; page 12-13: ©Seita, ©Jose Breton- Pics Action / Shutterstock.com; page 14-15: ©sArhange1, ©Arne Dedert, ©Jose Breton- Pics Action; page 16-17: ©Thanongsak Yinnaitham / Shutterstock.com, ©Chuck Myers; page 18-19: ©Anne-Marie Sorvin; page 20: ©Michael Chow; page 21: ©Jose Breton- Pics Action / Shutterstock.com; page 22-23: ©Pierre Teyssot / Shutterstock.com, ©Romain Biard / Shutterstock.com; page 24-25: ©Sam Simmonds; page 26-27: ©Tendo23, ©Represented by ZUMA Press, Inc.; page 28: ©bombuscreative; page 29: ©Richard Buxo / SplashNews

Edited by: Madison Capitano
Cover and interior design by: Rhea Magaro-Wallace

Library of Congress PCN Data

Megan Rapinoe / Mary Hertz Scarbrough
(Women in Sports)
ISBN 978-1-73163-823-6 (hard cover)
ISBN 978-1-73163-900-4 (soft cover)
ISBN 978-1-73163-977-6 (e-Book)
ISBN 978-1-73164-054-3 (ePub)
Library of Congress Control Number: 2020930168

Rourke Educational Media
Printed in the United States of America
01-1942011937